DISGUSTING & DREADFUL SCIENCE

Killer Plants
and other green gunk

by Anna Claybourne

 Crabtree Publishing Company
www.crabtreebooks.com

Crabtree Publishing Company
www.crabtreebooks.com
1-800-387-7650

Published in Canada
Crabtree Publishing
616 Welland Avenue
St. Catharines, ON
L2M 5V6

Published in the United States
Crabtree Publishing
PMB 59051
350 Fifth Ave, 59th Floor
New York, NY 10118

Printed in Hong Kong/082014/BK20140613

Author: Anna Claybourne
Editorial director: Kathy Middleton
Editor: Anastasia Suen
Proofreader: Wendy Scavuzzo
Prepress technician: Katherine Berti
Print and production coordinator: Katherine Berti

Produced by Penny Worms & Graham Rich, Book Packagers

Published by Crabtree Publishing Company in 2015

First published in 2014 by Franklin Watts
(a division of Hachette Children's Books)
Copyright © Franklin Watts 2014

Picture acknowledgements:
123rf.com: 13tr (Dmitry Knorre), 15tr (Bonita Cheshier). **Alamy:** 17bl (Bajan Images). **Imaginechina/Corbis:** 22br. **iStockphoto.com:** title page (Dean Murray), eyeball cartoon (Elaine Barker), 25br (sdominick) . **NASA:** 4tr. **New Line/Saul Zaentz/Wing Nut Films/The Kobal Collection/Vinet, Pierre:** 6t. **Prashanth NS/daktre.com:** 14b. **Shutterstock.com:** angry monster cartoon (Yayayoyo), cover (frog/Mark Bridger), cover (cactus/nayladen), 4b (BlueRingMedia), 4t (Zffoto), 5tl (Scott Prokop), 5b (Memo Angeles), 5tr (Sedlacek), 6bl (Andreas Meyer), 7r (Kathy Gold), 8t (Arcady), 8b (Kirsanov Valerly Vladimirovich), 8cr (Hein Nouwens), 8cl (L Skywalker), 9tr (Dimijana), 9m (Banprik), 9bl (rosedesigns), 9br (picturepartners), 10t (Tatiana Volgutova) 10 close up (Bildagentur Zoonar GmbH) 11b (Jean Valley), 11c (David Pusey), 12t (Micimakin), 12b (Kolesov Sergei), 13c (Pejo), 13bl (Viktar Malyshchyts), 13br (S J Watt), 14t (Lee Prince), 15cr (turkkub), 15br (Shelli Jensen), 16t (carroteater), 16b (Kazakov Maksim), 16b (poison ivy leaf/Steven Russell Smith Photos), 17tr (cow/Pixel Memoirs), 17tl (Igor Stramyk), 18bl (Anan Kaewkhammul), 18br (hypnotype), 19t (Phase4Studios), 19cl (Madlen), 19cr (MaraZe), 20l and cover (Cathy Keifer), 20br, 21br (Pakhnyushcha), 22c (Julia M. Fotografie), 23c (BMJ), 24t (Heike Brauer), 24b (blambca), 25tr (Zorandim), 25c (Ase), 25bl (Miriam Doerr), 26tr and cover (Muhd Azim Yusof), 26cl (Paul Rommer), 26cr (Antonio S), 26bl (Kokhanchikov), 27b (aa3), 28t (Pablo Scapinachis), 28b (Georgy Markov), 29 (Wood/Ed Samuel), 29 (cotton/Aaron Amat), 29 (cork/D7INAMI7S), 29 (paper/LiliGraphie), 29 (elastic/Ilya Akinshin), 29br (velirina). **Tom Le Mesurier/Eat Rio:** 26br. **Wikimedia:** 21tr, 23br (KeresH). **Wikipedia:** cover (red seeds/Steve Hurst @ USDA), 6br, 7tl (J W Buel), 11t, 17tr (giant hogweed/Henry Clark), 17br (HansHillewaert/CC-BY-SA-3.0), 23tl, 27tr (Fritzflohrreynolds).

All other illustrations by Graham Rich

Every attempt has been made to clear copyright. Should there be any inadvertent omission, please apply to the publisher for rectification.

Library and Archives Canada Cataloguing in Publication

Claybourne, Anna, author
    Killer plants and other green gunk / Anna Claybourne.

(Disgusting & dreadful science)
Includes index.
Issued in print and electronic formats.
ISBN 978-0-7787-1400-2 (bound).--ISBN 978-0-7787-1421-7 (pbk.).--
ISBN 978-1-4271-9355-1 (pdf).--ISBN 978-1-4271-9351-3 (html)

    1. Dangerous plants--Juvenile literature. 2. Carnivorous plants--Juvenile literature. 3. Plant defenses--Juvenile literature. I. Title.

QK100.A1C53 2014   j581.6'5   C2014-903947-6
    C2014-903948-4

Library of Congress Cataloging-in-Publication Data

Claybourne, Anna.
  Killer plants and other green gunk / by Anna Claybourne.
    pages cm. -- (Disgusting & dreadful science)
  Includes index.
  ISBN 978-0-7787-1400-2 (reinforced library binding) -- ISBN 978-0-7787-1421-7 (pbk.) --
ISBN 978-1-4271-9355-1 (electronic pdf) -- ISBN 978-1-4271-9351-3 (electronic html)
  1. Plant defenses--Juvenile literature. 2. Dangerous plants--Juvenile literature. I. Title.
II. Series: Claybourne, Anna. Disgusting & dreadful science.

QK921.C53 2014
581.4--dc23

    2014022790

Contents

Green, growing, and deadly!

Plants may seem mostly harmless. They can't chase you, catch you or eat you (...can they?). But plants actually have all kinds of scary secrets. While some simply strangle their neighbors or snap up flies, others are waiting to poison you, sting you, splat you with slimy goo – or merely engulf and destroy your house. Watch out – the plants are coming!

Earth's continents look green from space. Why? It's all those plants.

Plant planet

We humans may think we rule the Earth, but it's really a plant world. On land, plants actually outweigh animals by 1,000 to 1!

Plant parts

Most plants have the same basic parts.

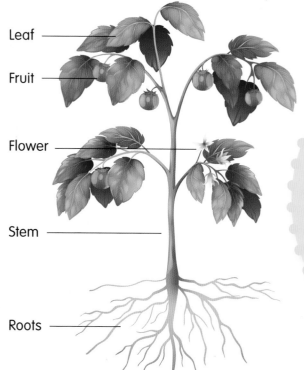

Leaf

Fruit

Flower

Stem

Roots

What is a plant?

Plants are living things that use light energy – usually from the Sun – to survive. They collect this energy in their leaves, and use it to help them turn water and gases from the air into the food they need to grow – a process called photosynthesis. Clever!

Unlike most animals, plants stay in one place. They have roots that reach down into the soil, and can collect all the sunlight, gases, and water they need without having to move around.

Plant POWER

Though plants grow and move slowly, they are tough and determined. They didn't get where they are today by being easily beaten! Weeds will spring up wherever they can, tree roots can push through pavement, and grass survives being trampled by millions of feet. Given enough time, plants will completely surround and overgrow anything in their way.

Deadly weapons

Staying still means plants can't run away from danger. They're always at risk of being eaten, squashed or cut down. So they've developed an arsenal of amazing weapons to defend themselves – from killer poisons and painful **venom** injections to giant, razor-sharp thorns. And a few plants go one step further – they catch and eat animals!

Yum, Yum...

Ouch!

Ever been stung by a nettle? Well that's just the start! Turn the page to discover the world's disgusting and dreadful plants and what they might do to you...

Terrible tales

Enter the world of films and fairy tales, myths and legends, and you'll encounter some truly terrifying plant monsters. Most real plants aren't THIS scary – but sometimes there's a grain of truth in their magical powers.

Talking trees

In J R R Tolkien's *Lord of the Rings*, walking, talking tree giants called the Ents are gentle and kind guardians of the forest. But according to hobbits Pippin and Merry (right) "their punches can crumple iron like tinfoil, and they can tear apart solid rock like breadcrusts." And when the forest is threatened, they get extremely angry...

Who said that?

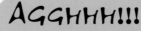

AGGHHH!!!

Magical mandrake

Since ancient times, the mandrake plant, or mandragora, has been renowned for its medicinal and magical effects. Its root was said to look like a human body, and people believed the plant screamed when pulled out of the ground. In fact, the roots are poisonous and **hallucinogenic**, meaning they can make you see things that aren't really there. This could explain the plant's magical reputation.

Man-eaters

According to old legends, and a few adventure novels, trees that could eat humans were said to grow on the island of Madagascar, off the east coast of Africa. The tree was sometimes given the creepy name "Ya-te-veo" meaning "I see you" – yikes! It was believed to reach out with its snake-like branches to grab people and gobble them up.

Yikes!

These plant tales may not be true, but there are plants that eat animals and others that have damaging and sometimes fatal effects on humans... as you'll soon discover!

Other plants to avoid...

1
The Whomping Willow
This frightening tree in the Harry Potter books thrashes around and attacks anyone who comes too close.

2
The Triffids
These are terrifying walking plants with whip-like branches that sting and kill. They were created in a book by John Wyndham in 1951.

3
The Lotus Tree
In Greek mythology, the fruit of the mysterious Lotus tree made anyone who ate it forget everything about their lives.

Deadly poison

There are hundreds of plants that contain enough poison to be deadly to anyone who accidentally eats them. Even worse, some of them have been used to kill people on purpose! Long ago, poisoning was a popular murder method, and plants played a big part.

Wolf-killer

The aconite plant is famous for its powerful poison. One aconite plant is called "wolfsbane" because it was once used to kill wolves. It appears as a poison in an ancient Greek legend, when the evil queen Medea tries to get rid of Theseus with an aconite-laced drink. **Apothecaries** in medieval times used it to make poisons for killing rats and other pests – or sometimes, human enemies!

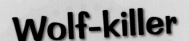

We're pretty...

...deadly!

Another aconite plant is called "monkshood," because its flowers look like long, droopy hoods.

Parsnip peril

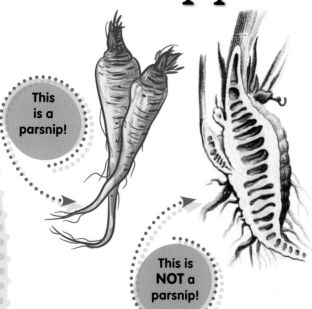

This is a parsnip!

This is NOT a parsnip!

Water hemlock or "wild parsnip" has killed some people who thought its roots were real parsnips. As you can imagine, it's a very bad idea to eat any plant you find growing in the wild.

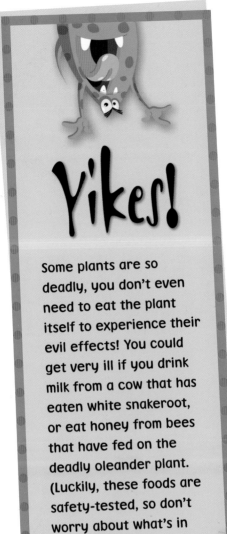

Yikes!

Some plants are so deadly, you don't even need to eat the plant itself to experience their evil effects! You could get very ill if you drink milk from a cow that has eaten white snakeroot, or eat honey from bees that have fed on the deadly oleander plant. (Luckily, these foods are safety-tested, so don't worry about what's in your fridge.)

Deadly beans

The deadliest plant poisons of all are found in two bean-like seeds: castor beans (right) and rosary peas (below). Strangely, the same seeds are used as beads to make jewelry, and to make castor oil, which is harmless. But if the poison is extracted from the seeds, just a tiny amount of it can kill.

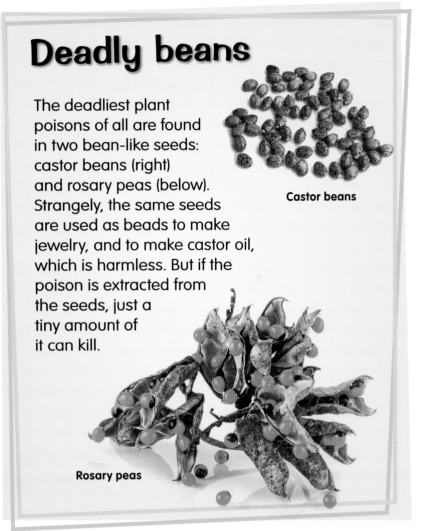

Castor beans

Rosary peas

Open wide!

Why would anyone put poison in their eyes? Women used to do this with the juice of the extremely poisonous deadly nightshade plant. It made their pupils **dilate**, or open wide, which they thought made them look prettier. Unfortunately, it also damaged their eyesight. The plant is also called belladonna, Italian for "pretty lady."

Deadly nightshade – the clue is in the name!

Stingers and stabbers

I f you were a plant, and a hungry rabbit, deer, or elephant was coming toward you, how would you get rid of it? Poison is one way but, by the time it works, it will be a bit too late for you. So lots of plants fight off their enemies with thorns, spikes, or painful injections.

Injections!?

Yes – some plants actually stick tiny needles into you, and pump in toxic chemicals. The best known example is the common, everyday stinging nettle. It's covered in tiny stinging hairs that are hollow, like hospital needles. Each has a bag of venom at the base, and a very fine, sharp tip.

When you brush against these needles, the tips break off and the venom flows into your skin. **Ouch!**

See for Yourself

Sting study

To get a good look at a nettle's stings, collect a nettle plant – wearing thick gardening gloves – and use a magnifying glass to spot the stinging "needles". Don't put your nose too close!

Monster nettle

Not scared of nettles? Meet New Zealand's giant tree nettle, which has huge stingers, super-strong venom, and can grow to 16 feet (5 meters) tall! Its stings are so powerful, they can be deadly – even to humans.

The thorn tree

The thorns of the African acacia tree don't contain venom – they are just sharp spikes. They deter some animals from grazing on the small, juicy leaves. But, unfortunately for the acacia, a giraffe's tongue is tough and agile – and their favorite lunch is acacia leaves!

Yikes!

Any thorn can be dangerous if it stabs deeply and gives you an infection. Even rose thorns have caused deadly illnesses. If you ever get a deep wound from a plant thorn, go to the doctor!

Cruel cactus

Some types of cactus have barbed spines that are almost impossible to pull out once they get stuck in your skin. Meanwhile, their smaller, hair-like spines detach from the plant, float around in the air, and can damage your eyes.

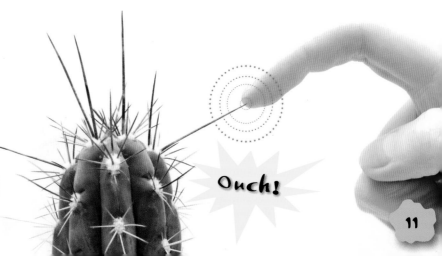

Ouch!

11

Squirters and splatters

Imagine you're relaxing in a lawn chair in a sunny garden, when suddenly: Pop! SPLAT! Something slimy, sloppy, and gloopy lands on your head!

Splatted with fruit

Fruit trees don't sound dangerous, but they can splat pavements, roads, and cars with ripe fruit, which then rots and goes slimy and slippery. Rotting fruit even causes accidents when people slip and slide on it.

Seed spreading

Why do plants squirt and splat? It's usually to do with their fruits and seeds, which drop off, or sometimes fly, pop, or squirt into the air. They do this so that they can land in the soil, and grow into a new plant. Often, the seeds are surrounded by jelly-like slime. This dampens the soil and helps the seeds to germinate, or start growing.

Yuck!

Some plants have a revolting but clever way of spreading their seeds far and wide. They grow tasty fruits or berries, which are eaten by animals and birds. The seeds of the fruits travel through the guts and come out in the animals' poop, ready to grow into new plants.

Exploding cucumber

3... **2...** **1...**  BLAST OFF!

The farther a plant can fling its seeds, the wider its **species** will spread. So some plants, such as the squirting cucumber, explode with a SPLAT! to shoot their seeds, and the slimy gloop around them, far and wide.

A ripe, ready-to-pop squirting cucumber looks like this...

Seed shooters

Some plants aren't quite so slimy, but still explode to scatter or disperse their seeds as far as they can. When Himalayan balsam seed pods pop, you can hear a clicking sound, and the seeds shoot up to 23 feet (7 meters) away!

 ## See for Yourself

Lychee

Slimy or squirty?

Buy some or all of the fruits in the table to the right. Then do a slime and squirt test by touching and squeezing the flesh or seeds inside. The riper the fruit, the better! Then grade the fruits from 1 to 5 – with 5 being the slimiest and squirtiest.

SHOPPING LIST
Pomegranate
Custard apple
Lychee
Passion fruit
Mango

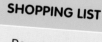

Passion fruit

Scary stranglers

Most plants get the food and energy they need from the soil, water, air, and sunshine. This means they can live quite happily by themselves. But parasitic plants have developed a different way of surviving. They attach themselves to another plant, and suck food and water out of them instead. Sometimes, they suck and strangle them to death!

Sneaky strangler

The strangler fig, found in tropical jungles, gets its name because it wraps itself around another tree, called the **host** tree. The strangler uses the host as a support so its leaves can reach up to the sunlight on the treetops. Meanwhile, its roots grow around the host and reach down to the soil.

A strangler fig strangling an unlucky cypress tree.

Eventually, the host tree can become completely surrounded. The roots are strangled, and the tree dies and rots away. In the meantime, the strangler fig has created its own "trunk" to hold it up, which is just a hollow tube.

Strangling a house!

Some types of strangler figs grow around houses or walls and can overwhelm them if they are not stopped. A creeping fig can totally cover a house so it looks like a giant hedge!

The dodder is also called devil's hair, witches' hair, devil's guts, or strangleweed.

I'll sniff you out!

The spooky dodder vine is an orange stringy parasitic plant that tangles itself around its hosts and feeds on them. It can sense chemicals in the air from other plants, and grow toward the ones it likes, such as a juicy tomato or potato plant. Once it grabs onto its host, it loses its roots, as it doesn't need them any more. Slurp!

Ouch!

Instead of having their roots in the soil, some parasitic plants have scary haustoria that pierce the host plant. This is how they suck out the water and food they need.

Tree home

The mistletoe plant never needs to touch the ground at all. It grows high in a tree, sucking up the tree's food and water. It spreads from one tree to another when birds eat the mistletoe berries. The seeds come out in the birds' poop, landing on other trees' branches.

15

skin attackers

If you touch the leaves of the poison ivy plant, you could end up with a painful, itchy rash or even big blisters. Ouch! The ivy releases a poison that sticks to your skin, and most people are sensitive to it. Poison ivy is found all across North America, and is just one of many plants worldwide that fight back against enemies with skin-damaging chemicals.

The rash appears 12 to 48 hours after the poison touches you, and can last for more than two weeks.

See for Yourself

Spot the poison ivy

It's useful to be able to spot dangerous plants – but could you spot poison ivy? It's actually not related to common ivy, and looks quite innocent.
Look out for:

• Smooth and shiny leaves

• Mid-to-dark green

• 3 leaves with pointed tips on one stem.

   Which is it?
   (Answer below.)

Answer: 4

BEWARE GIANT HOGWEED

Delicious

Giant hogweed looks like a huge version of an everyday weed, with pretty, umbrella-like white flowers. But it has a secret weapon – dangerous **sap** that is activated by sunlight. If you get it on your skin and the sun shines on it, it can cause huge, burning blisters and deep wounds that can last for years. If you get it in your eyes, it can even cause blindness!

Strangely, cows, pigs, and other farm animals seem to be immune to the effects of giant hogweed.

Murderous manchineel

The manchineel tree, found in the Americas, is one of the most deadly trees in the world. Its sap makes your skin blister and burn at the slightest touch. In fact, it's so poisonous, you can even get hurt by standing under the tree when it's raining, or from breathing the smoke when manchineel wood is burning.

Don't touch!

In some parts of the Caribbean, manchineel trees have warning signs or red paint on them to tell people to stay away.

Ouch!

Manchineel fruits look like small apples. They are nicknamed "manzanilla de la muerte" or "little death apple". Visitors sometimes eat them by mistake, and end up with blistering and swelling in their throats.

Clever tricks

Recent science shows plants are smarter than we thought. They may not be able to walk, but they can talk! It turns out that some trees can actually send messages to each other using chemical signals. Some plants may even be able to hear.

Kudu killers

After herds of African kudu antelopes died mysteriously, scientists discovered the mystery killer was... acacia trees! When antelopes or giraffes nibble the trees, the leaves release a chemical called ethylene that blows away on the wind. Other acacias detect it and start filling their leaves with bitter tannin to put the leaf-munchers off.

Animals normally leave the bad-tasting leaves uneaten, but the kudu that died were fenced in, so had no choice but to eat them.

Oh no! Now I have to be wary of hunters, big cats, AND acacia trees!

Caterpillar alert

Willow trees do something similar when they get eaten by caterpillars. They release chemicals that warn other trees nearby to make their own leaves taste bad.

18

Ouch!

Blue gum eucalyptus trees have a sinister way of wiping out rival plants. They create the perfect conditions for a forest fire with their piles of dry leaves and flammable oil, that can be easily sparked by lightning. Afterward, the tree regenerates and its seeds grow – helping the eucalyptus species to take over large areas.

Thanks for being there, Basil.

Who said that?

Can plants hear?

Gardeners know that some plants help each other to grow, while others don't. For example, chili plants grow better if basil is nearby. In experiments, scientists separated the plants with black plastic to stop chemical signals, but the effect still happened. This means plants may actually detect tiny sound vibrations from each other's **cells**.

See for Yourself

Take the plant test

Some gardeners claim plants grow better if you talk to them or play them music. To test this, grow two groups of seeds (such as sunflower seeds) in the same soil, in the same sized pots, with the same amount of water and sunlight – but chat or play music to just one group. Do they grow differently?

Meat-eaters

Uh oh!

Though it may sound like a horror story, some plants really do eat meat. But why? Most plants get their food and energy from air, water, and sunlight. However, they also need some nutrients, or food chemicals, from the soil. Carnivorous (meat-eating) plants usually grow in soggy bogs or on rocky slopes, where there's a shortage of soil nutrients – so they make up the difference by hunting.

Jaws and teeth

The most famous meat-eater is the Venus flytrap, that catches flies and other small insects in special traps formed from its leaves. They can close quickly like jaws, and have toothed edges that act like a cage to keep the fly inside.

Once trapped, the plant releases juices to dissolve the fly and soak it up. **Slurp!**

Don't panic!

These meat-eaters may sound ferocious, but even the fastest-moving carnivorous plants work quite slowly. It takes them days or weeks to dissolve and **digest** their prey. They can't harm humans, and won't bite your finger off!

Sticky traps

Sundew plants trap their prey using tentacles covered with blobs of sticky glue. Once an insect is stuck, the tentacle can curl over to trap it.

Slippery sides

Pitcher plants have a different kind of trap – tall, slippery-sided jug-shaped "pitchers" full of liquid. Insects, lizards, and other small animals that go too near the edge quickly fall in and can't escape. Then the gloopy liquid dissolves and digests them – sometimes leaving just a skeleton.

This lizard is discovering that the inside of a pitcher plant is extremely smooth and slippery.

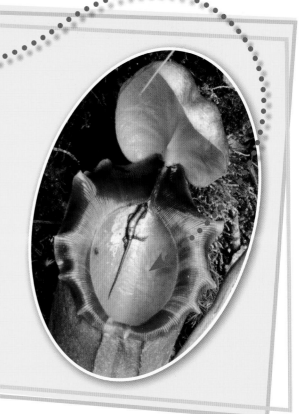

Water trap

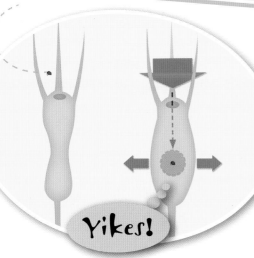

Yikes!

Bladderworts live in water or soggy soil. They have underwater traps with a vacuum (empty space) inside, and a tiny trap door with trigger hairs. When prey touches the hairs, the door springs inward and water is sucked inside, and the prey is sucked in with it. Genius!

Yuck!

The ultimate meat-eater is the giant pitcher plant. Its pitchers are up to 12 inches (30 cm), and have been known to trap rats!

Disgusting and deadly slime

One of the most revolting plant products is the slippery slime found in and around some fruits, seeds, and water weeds. But this slime isn't just disgusting – it can sometimes be deadly, too.

Pond slime

What is that gross, stringy slime that you can pick up out of a pond with a stick? It's a type of slimy algae – microscopic plant-like creatures – called spirogyra, that grows in long strands. Spirogyra can be bad news for pond life. If there's too much of it, other water plants can be choked by it. Water insects and fish can also find it hard to breathe and grow.

Croak!

Slimy seas

In some parts of the world, seas and lakes can turn red, brown, or a strange greenish color, thanks to an invasion of plant-like slime. This is called an algal bloom, and it's caused by billions of algae taking over an area of water. The algae are sometimes horribly harmful, releasing chemicals that kill sea creatures and poison shellfish on the beach.

Bird-catching tree

The bird-catching tree of Hawaii and New Zealand has such slimy, sticky fruits, that small birds regularly get stuck in them! However the tree doesn't trap the birds on purpose, and it doesn't eat them. Instead, the stickiness probably helps the fruits to stick to larger animals and birds such as seagulls, which then carry them away. This helps the seeds to disperse, or spread out.

Green fur

Would you like to have slimy algae growing on you? Probably not, but sloths do. Their fur is often green from all the algae growing in it, which they "catch" from their mom at a young age. In exchange for a home to live on, the algae provides the sloth with camouflage among the leafy treetops.

Thanks, Mom!

Yuck!

If you see something like THIS on the ground, it's probably a slime mold (a type of fungus). This bright yellow species has the attractive name "dog vomit." Or it could actually BE dog vomit!

Potent plants

Did you know that some plants contain drugs? "Drugs" can mean useful medicines such as aspirin, first discovered in willow tree bark, or harmful drugs such as heroin, which is made from a type of poppy. In fact, a drug is any chemical that changes the way the body works – and many of the most important drugs in the world come from plants.

Foxgloves look pretty, but avoid touching them!

Helpful or harmful?

Sometimes, a dangerous plant poison can also be a helpful medicine, depending on how much of it you use. For example, foxgloves contain a deadly poison that can kill by stopping the heart. But, in much smaller amounts, the same poison is used to make a medicine called digitalis that can slow down the heart if it is beating too fast.

Yuck!

Ipecacuanha, a plant from Brazil, contains a powerful emetic - a drug that makes you throw up! It was once used as a medicine to help people vomit after accidentally eating something poisonous.

Bleurgh!

Addictive plants

Addiction means becoming dependent on a drug, so that you have to take it all the time to avoid feeling ill. Tobacco, the plant used to make cigarettes, contains one of the most addictive drugs of all – nicotine.

Tobacco is not illegal, but many addictive drugs are. However, there's still a huge demand for them, and farmers in many parts of the world grow drug-producing crops.

A tobacco farmer tending his crop.

Cigarettes are made of tobacco leaves rolled up inside a paper tube. Breathing in the smoke delivers the addictive nicotine into your blood.

Everyday drugs

Even chocolate contains a drug! It's called theobromine, which can make your heart beat faster and make you feel more awake. Caffeine, found in coffee, is similar. Both these drugs come from the bean-like seeds of small, bushy trees. People everywhere love chocolate and coffee, so growing and manufacturing them is a huge business worldwide.

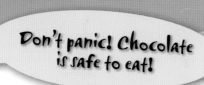

Don't panic! Chocolate is safe to eat!

What IS that SMELL?

Roses, jasmine, lilac, and honeysuckle are known for their beautiful sweet scents – and many flowers are used to make perfumes. But that's not the whole story – because there are some plants that smell DISGUSTING!

Rafflesia

Rotting meat

The stinkiest plants – to a human nose – are the ones that smell of rotting, putrid meat. Rafflesia and Titan arum, two of the world's largest flowers, both smell like this – and both have the charming nickname "corpse flower."

However, they don't smell bad enough to put animals off – in fact just the opposite. In the same way that sweet smells attract bees to other flowers, the smell of dead meat attracts flies to the stinky Rafflesia and Titan arum. As the insects move from one flower to another, they take the plants' pollen with them. This pollinates the plants, helping them to make seeds.

Isn't a corpse a dead body?

I love that smell!

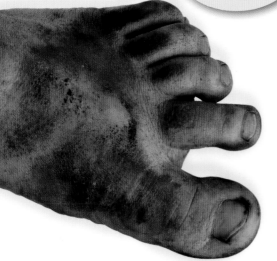

Smelly toes

The seed pods of the stinking toe tree look like large toes, and smell like stinky feet!

Stinking toe tree pods

Skunk cabbage

It doesn't look like a skunk or a cabbage, but it smells as bad as both! Skunk cabbage takes its name from one of the smelliest animals on the planet. The smell attracts flies or beetles to spread the plant's pollen.

Skunk cabbage isn't that nice to look at either!

| No smoking | No eating or drinking |
| No flammable goods | No durians |

The smell of durians is so revolting that eating them on public transportation is banned in some countries.

Ban the fruit!

It's not just flowers that smell – the durian, popular in southeast Asia, is a super-smelly fruit. Many people love the taste, but everyone agrees it smells terrible – like a mixture of smelly socks, dirty toilets, and rotting onions!

Ouch!

Durians are killers, too! People have died from eating too much (causing a build-up of harmful chemicals), or when the huge spiky fruits fell from the tree onto their heads.

A durian cut in half, revealing the soft (and smelly) flesh inside the spiky shell.

It's not all bad

So, plants can sting you, stab you, poison you, prickle you, or squirt you with slime – not to mention catch and eat passing animals. But don't write them off just yet! Plants are actually incredibly important to us – essential, in fact. Even the scary, slimy ones...

Jungles and forests keep the air fresh.

No plants, no food

We couldn't live without plants, because they are at the bottom of the food chain – the sequence of living things that survive by feeding on each other.

Most humans are omnivores, meaning we eat both plant and animal foods. But even animal-based foods only exist thanks to plants.

Fresh air

If it weren't for plants, we wouldn't just starve – we'd suffocate! When humans and other animals breathe, we take in oxygen gas from the air, and breathe out carbon dioxide gas. Plants do the opposite. Their leaves take in carbon dioxide, and give out oxygen. This keeps the gases in the Earth's **atmosphere** balanced.

I love being an omnivore!

Plants grow by using sunlight, air, nutrients, and water (plus the occasional fly!) to make plant parts. These plant parts – leaves, flowers, nuts, fruits, and roots – become food for plant-eating animals. And plant-eating animals are food for meat-eating animals. Without plants, the whole food chain would fall apart.

Plants products

Besides food and oxygen, plants give us all kinds of other useful things. Which of these plant products have you used recently?

PAPER
made from wood

CORK
from the bark of the cork tree

WOOD
from tree trunks and branches

COTTON
from the fluffy seed coverings of the cotton plant

RUBBER
from the sap of the rubber tree

See for Yourself

Plant parts

Look at this list of fruit and vegetables. Which part of the plant are they – fruits, seeds, flowers, stems, or roots?

BROCCOLI, CARROT, RHUBARB, MANGO, PEAS, CHILI, POTATO

What am I?

Answers: Broccoli - flowers, carrot - root, rhubarb - stem, mango - fruit, peas - seeds, chili - fruit, potato - root

Glossary

addictive causing a need to have the same thing regularly

algae microscopic plant-like living things that usually make their own food

apothecaries old-fashioned makers and sellers of medicines and poisons

aspirin a type of painkiller

atmosphere the layer of gases surrounding Earth

cells the tiny units that living things are made up of

digest to break down food into useful chemicals and soak them up

dilate to get wider

disperse to spread out over a wide area

energy the power that nutrients from food provide to the body

fungus a type of living thing that includes molds and mushrooms. Fungi are not plants, but can sometimes look similar.

germinate to start to grow

hallucinogenic causing hallucinations, or visions of things that aren't real

haustoria fine root-like parts found on parasitic plants, used to suck food and water from the host

heroin a highly addictive, illegal drug made from a type of poppy

host a plant or other living thing that a parasite lives on

infection an invasion of germs into a living thing

nutrients found in food, nutrients help living things grow and stay healthy

omnivore living thing that eats both plants and animals

parasitic surviving by living in or on another living thing and its food

photosynthesis the process plants use to make food using sunlight

pollen powdery substance produced by plants as part of making seeds

pollinates spreads pollen from one plant to another of the same species

sap liquid that flows around inside a plant

species a particular type of living thing

venom the poison in the bite or sting of some animals

Websites and Places to visit

Plants for Kids
www.sciencekids.co.nz/plants.html
Plant games, quizzes, projects, and pictures.

Biology4Kids: Plants
www.biology4kids.com/files/plants_main.
html
Useful basic plant facts and science.

Simple Plant Science Experiments
www.livescience.com/43560-plant-science-
for-kids.html
A selection of plant experiments to try.

Science & Plants for Schools
www.saps.org.uk/primary/teaching-
resources/199-having-fun-growing-plants
Plant-growing and gardening activities and
projects to try.

The Eden Project
Bodelva, St Austell, Cornwall, PL24 2SG, UK
www.edenproject.com

The New York Botanical Garden
2900 Southern Blvd.
Bronx, NY 10458-5126
www.nybg.org

Redwood National and State Parks
c/o Crescent City Information Center
1111 Second Street, Crescent City, CA
www.nps.gov/redw

Royal Botanical Gardens, Ontario, Canada
680 Plains Road West
Burlington, ON, Canada
www.rbg.ca

Royal Botanical Gardens, Edinburgh
20A Inverleith Row
Edinburgh EH3 5LR, UK
http://www.rbge.org.uk

Royal Botanic Gardens, Kew
Kew, Richmond, Surrey, TW9 3AB, UK
www.kew.org

Index